IF YOU MADE
A MILLION

CHEERFUL AND WILLING
HELPERS
WANTED
by MARVELOSISSIMO
THE MATHEMATICAL MAGICIAN

LOTHROP, LEE & SHEPARD BOOKS   New York

Text copyright © 1989 by David M. Schwartz
Illustrations copyright © 1989 by Steven Kellogg
Photographs of money copyright © 1989 by George Ancona

First Edition   1 2 3 4 5 6 7 8 9 10

Library of Congress Cataloging in Publication Data
Schwartz, David M. If you made a million / by David M. Schwartz; pictures by Steven Kellogg.
  p.   cm.   Summary: Describes the various forms which money can take, including coins, paper money, and personal checks, and how it can be used to make purchases, pay off loans, or build interest in the bank.
  ISBN 0-688-07017-5.   ISBN 0-688-07018-3 (lib. bdg.)   1. Finance, Personal—Juvenile literature.   [1. Finance, Personal. 2. Money.]   I. Kellogg, Steven, ill.   II. Title. HG179.S335 1989 332.024—dc19
88-12819 CIP AC

IF YOU MADE A MILLION

by David M. Schwartz

pictures by Steven Kellogg

CONGRATULATIONS! YOU'VE EARNED A PENNY.

It will buy anything that costs one cent.

WELL DONE! YOU'VE MADE A NICKEL.

ONE NICKEL

is worth the same as FIVE PENNIES

HOORAY! NOW YOU HAVE A DIME.

ONE DIME

has the same value as TWO NICKELS

or TEN PENNIES

EXCELLENT! FOR YOUR HARD WORK YOU'VE EARNED A QUARTER.

ONE QUARTER

is the same amount of money as **FIVE NICKELS**

or **TWO DIMES AND ONE NICKEL**

or **THREE NICKELS AND ONE DIME**

or **TWENTY-FIVE PENNIES**

BLOW
UP
this
BOA
Earn 25¢

WONDERFUL! YOU ARE NOW A DOLLAR RICHER.

ONE DOLLAR

is worth as much as FOUR QUARTERS

FIX THIS
FOUNTAIN'S FLOW
· ·
Earn $1.

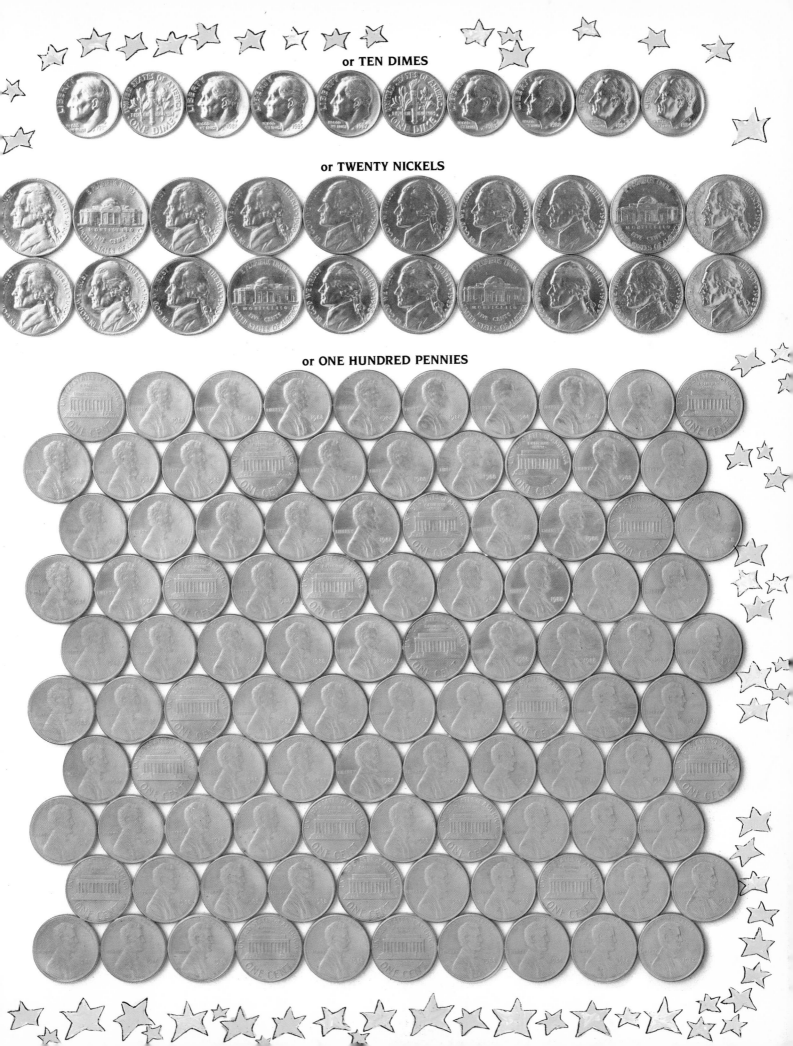

or TEN DIMES

or TWENTY NICKELS

or ONE HUNDRED PENNIES

You could use your dollar to buy
one hundred pieces of penny candy,

or twenty five-cent balloons,

or ten stickers for ten cents each,
or four rubber balls that cost
twenty-five cents apiece.

Or perhaps you'd like to save your dollar.
You could put it in the bank,
and a year from now it will be worth $1.05.

The bank wants to use your money,
and it will pay you five cents
to leave your dollar there for a year.
The extra five cents is called interest.

If you waited ten years, your dollar would earn
sixty-four cents in interest just from sitting in the bank.

Are you interested in earning lots of interest? Wait
twenty years, and one dollar will grow to $2.70.

DELICIOUS! YOU'VE BAKED A CAKE
AND EARNED FIVE DOLLARS.

You could be paid with one five-dollar bill

or five one-dollar bills. It doesn't matter.
They have the same value.

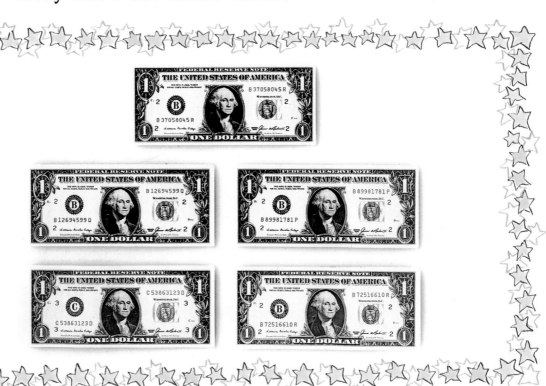

STUPENDOUS! YOU'VE MADE TEN DOLLARS.
How would you like to be paid?
One ten-dollar bill? Two five-dollar bills?
Ten one-dollar bills?
Or perhaps one five and five ones?
Take your pick—they're all worth ten dollars.

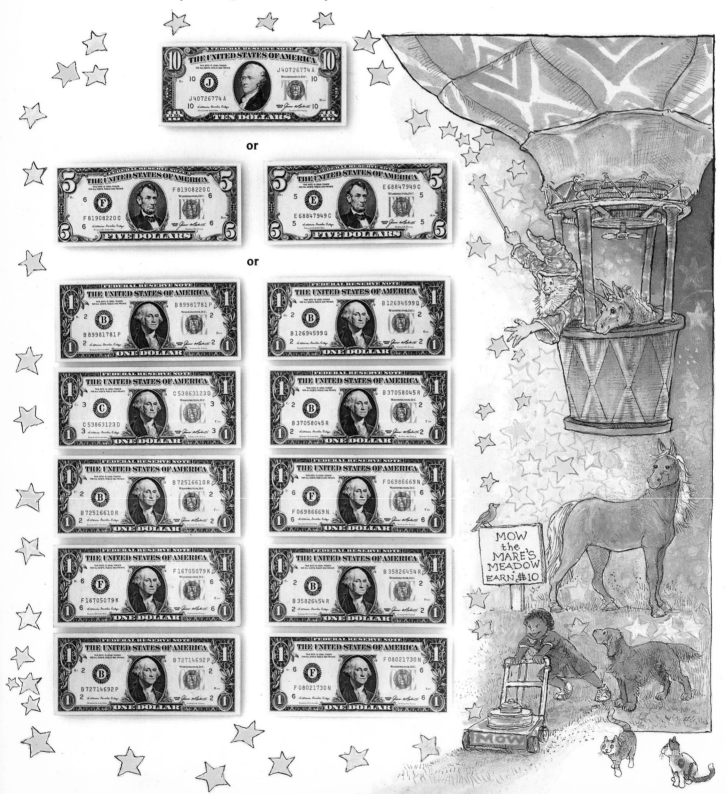

If you prefer coins, you can have
a five-foot stack of pennies
(that's one thousand of them) or
a fifteen-inch stack of two hundred nickels.
You could also be paid with one hundred dimes,
which would stack up to just over five inches.
Or you can receive your ten dollars
as a 3¹/₄-inch pile of forty quarters.

You could spend your ten dollars on ten kittens
or one thousand kitty snacks.

Or you could take your mom to the movies.

But maybe you'd rather save your money.
If you leave your ten dollars in the bank
for ten years, it will earn $6.40 in interest,
and you will have $16.40.

If you leave it there for fifty years,
your ten dollars will grow to $138.02.

YOU'VE WORKED HARD TO EARN ONE HUNDRED DOLLARS.
You've decided to spend it on a plane ticket
to the beach. You could pay with
a hundred-dollar bill, or two fifty-dollar bills,
or five twenty-dollar bills, or many other
combinations—
six fives, three tens, and two twenties, for instance.

Paying with pennies?
You'll need ten thousand of them,
and they'll make a fifty-foot stack.

YOU'VE WORKED LONG AND HARD,
AND YOU'VE EARNED A THOUSAND DOLLARS!
You're going to buy a pet.

You could pay with coins or bills.

If you don't like the idea of carrying
a thousand dollars around with you,
you can put it in the bank
and pay for the hippo with a check.

The check tells your bank to give $1,000
to the person who sold you the hippo.

GRACE
CHEERFUL AND WILLING INC.
Somewhere, U.S.A.

Pay to the
order of ___ MR. HORACE HUGGABLE ___ $1,000.00

___ ONE THOUSAND and 0/100 Dollars

Grace

THE BANK
Somewhere, U.S.A.

Here's how it works: You give the check
to the person who sold you the hippo,
and he gives it to his bank,
and his bank sends it to a very busy
clearinghouse in the city,
and the clearinghouse tells your bank
to take $1,000 out of your money.

After your bank does that,
the clearinghouse tells the hippo salesman's bank
to add $1,000 to his money, so he can take it
and use it whenever, and however, he likes.
Maybe he'll use it to raise more hippos.

If you used pennies to purchase
a $10,000 Ferris wheel,
someone might not be too happy about it.
Even if you used ten thousand one-dollar bills,
they would be mighty hard to handle.

Probably a check would be best.

MAGNIFICENT! YOU'VE EARNED $50,000.
And you've just read about
a well-worn, unloved, but perfectly fixable
castle for sale. The price: $100,000.

The castle costs $100,000 and you have only $50,000.
You're $50,000 short, but you can still buy the castle.
You could use the money you earned as a down payment
and ask a bank to lend you the rest.

Then you would pay the bank back,
a little at a time, month after month...

for many years.

But the amount you must pay the bank
will be *more* than what you borrowed.
That's because the bank charges
for lending you money. The extra money
is called interest, just like the interest
the bank pays to you when it uses your money.
Now you are using the bank's money, so you must
pay interest to the bank.

If you have some very expensive plans,
you may have to take on a tough job
that pays well.

If you think ogre-taming would be
an exciting challenge, you can have fun
and make a great deal of money, too.
Of course, you may not enjoy
taming obstreperous ogres or building bulky bridges
or painting purple pots. Enjoying your work
is more important than money, so you should look
for another job or make less expensive plans.

CONGRATULATIONS! YOU'VE MADE A MILLION.

A MILLION DOLLARS!
That's a stack of pennies ninety-five miles high,
or enough nickels to fill a school bus,
or a whale's weight in quarters.

Would you prefer your million in paper money?
Even a paper million is a hefty load:
A million one-dollar bills would weigh 2,500 pounds
and stack up to 360 feet.

What's the smallest your million could be?
One-hundred-dollar bills are the largest made today,
and it would take ten thousand of them
to pay you for your feat of ogre-taming.
But a check for $1,000,000
would easily fit in your pocket or purse.
And it's worth the same as the towering stacks
of pennies or bills.

Now you can afford to buy tickets to the moon.

Or you can purchase some real estate
for the endangered rhinoceroses.

But if you'd rather save your million
than spend it, you could put it
in the bank, where it would earn interest.
The interest on a million is about $1,000 a week,
or $143 a day, or $6 an hour, or 10 cents a minute.
Just from sitting in the bank!

If you keep your million, you can probably
live on the interest without doing any more work
for the rest of your life. You might like that,
or you could find it rather dull.

Making money means making choices.

SO WHAT WOULD YOU DO IF YOU MADE A MILLION?

A Note from the Author

What Would We Do Without Money?

It's difficult to imagine a world without money, but there was a time when money did not exist. If you had lived back then and you wanted to buy some beaver skins to make a coat, you would have had to barter, or trade, for them. Perhaps you raised goats. You might have bartered one goat for two skins. This may have worked out just fine some of the time, but it probably wasn't convenient to take your goats along every time you went shopping. And suppose you wanted only one beaver skin. You couldn't very well offer half a goat. People realized that bartering had its disadvantages, and eventually money was invented.

Money is anything that people agree to place a value on and use in trade for goods (like Ferris wheels) and services (like mowing meadows). Some of the objects that have been used as money may surprise you. The ancient Romans paid their soldiers in salt, and the Latin word for salt, *salarium*, is still with us as the modern English word "salary." Spices, cheese, shells, beans, silk, fishhooks, even gumdrops and woodpecker scalps have all been called money at one time or another. If you had lived in a place that used fishhooks as money, you could have sold a goat for, say, 500 fishhooks, and used 250 of them to buy a beaver skin.

It took many centuries before people started to exchange objects that we would recognize as money. Around 650 B.C., coins came into use. They were much easier to carry around than goats, and people were willing to accept their value because they were made from precious metals like copper, bronze, silver, and especially gold. But the problem with coins was that they could get mighty heavy if you were buying or selling something expensive.

In the middle of the thirteenth century, the Chinese solved this problem with paper money. The paper itself was not worth much, but the Chinese emperor who issued it said that it was to have a certain value, and his word was law. Instead of lugging heavy gold coins around, a Chinese person who wanted to buy something that cost ten pounds of gold could carry lightweight pieces of paper that the emperor said were worth the same as ten pounds of gold. (The emperor also said it was a crime for people to make their own pieces of paper that looked like money. This is called counterfeiting, and to be sure it didn't happen, the emperor printed a stern warning on his money: it said counterfeiting was punishable by death!)

Today national governments do the same thing as the Chinese emperor. In the United States, the government issues paper money worth one dollar, five dollars, ten, twenty, fifty, and one hundred dollars. (There used to be bills worth five hundred dollars, one thousand dollars, and more, all the way up to one hundred thousand, but they have been discontinued.) For amounts smaller than one dollar, the government issues coins. The common coins are pennies, nickels, dimes, and quarters.

(An occasional half-dollar or dollar coin turns up, but these are relatively rare.) The government, not the material the money is made from, determines its value.

Banks: They Don't Work Like Piggybanks

Everyone loves to spend his or her hard-earned money, but you may not want to spend yours right away. There are some good reasons to deposit it in a bank.

When you bring money to a bank, you can put it into a savings account or a checking account. If you intend to keep your money in the bank for a long time, you should put it in a savings account where it will actually grow. If you intend to use it by writing checks to pay for the things you want to buy (Ferris wheels or hippopotamuses, for example), or for the services you want people to perform (like fixing bridges or taming ogres), you should put it in a checking account.

When one of the Cheerful and Willing kids earns a dollar, he deposits it in a savings account at his bank. Although he hands the dollar to a man at the bank, his dollar doesn't sit there waiting for him to take it out later. Banks don't work like piggybanks! In a piggybank, your pennies wait patiently for you to dump them out, and when you finally do, you get the very same pennies you dropped into the pig. But when you deposit a penny (or a dollar or a million dollars) in a bank, you won't get the same penny (or dollar or million dollars) when you withdraw it later. That's because the bank has used your money.

The bank lends money to people who want to buy cars or houses, start businesses, or do other things that cost more than they have. The money that the bank lends to these people is the money you and others have deposited in savings accounts. To encourage people to save money in the bank, the bank pays them interest. To understand how interest payments work, you will need to understand fractions, decimals, and percentages. If you haven't yet learned about them, skip to Checks and Checking Accounts.

Interest and Compound Interest

You might wonder how much interest you'll earn if you put your money in a savings account. Many banks pay 5¼ percent annual (yearly) interest. If you deposited $100 at one of these banks, you might think that during one year you would earn $5.25 in interest, because 5¼% of $100 is $5.25. That would give you a total of $105.25 when added to your original $100 deposit. And you might think that during the second year your money would earn another $5.25 in interest, raising your $100 investment to $110.50 ($105.25 + $5.25 = $110.50). But banks actually pay more than this. They figure out their interest in a slightly different way so that your money earns what's called compound interest. Here's how compound interest works:

Let's imagine a bank that figures out your interest once a year. If you had deposited $100, you would earn $5.25 after one year, and your account would hold $105.25. During the second year you have $105.25, so the bank must pay 5¼% interest on

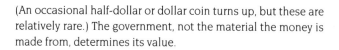

$105.25, which is $5.53. Notice that you've earned more interest the second year than you did the first because you are now earning interest on more money—not just your original $100, but also the $5.25 you made during the first year. In other words, you are earning interest on interest. That is what compound interest is all about—earning interest on interest.

With compound interest, after two years you have $110.78 ($100 + $5.25 + $5.53). In the third year you will earn 5¼% of $110.78, which is $5.81. Just as your second year's interest was larger than the first, your third year's interest is even larger than the second. Every year your interest will be larger than it was the year before. That is the magic of compound interest.

Actually, you won't have to wait a whole year before earning compound interest. Most banks figure out, or compound, your interest more often than that. Some banks compound interest four times a year (or quarterly), some every month (monthly), and some every day (daily). Let's look at interest on $100 that is compounded daily.

After just one day, your $100 will start to earn interest. How much? Well, the yearly interest rate is 5¼% and there are 365 days in a year, so in one day it would earn 1/365 of 5¼%, or 0.0143835% (5.25 ÷ 365) On $100, that's 1.43835 cents. This may not seem like much, but your money has been in the bank only one day! On the second day your money will earn a little bit more than it did the first day because it's worth a little bit more (due to the interest it earned during the first day). On the third day you'll make slightly more than that. And so on, until the end of the year. When you add up all 365 interest payments for the whole year, it comes out to $5.39.

Do you remember that you made $5.25 the first year when the bank figured your interest only once a year? Now, at a bank that compounds interest daily, you have earned $5.39. The difference is fourteen cents. True, fourteen cents isn't much, but the more money you deposit and the longer you wait, the more you will gain by having your interest compounded daily instead of just once a year. Suppose, for example, *you* tamed the obstreperous ogre and earned a million dollars! If you put it in a bank that compounds interest only once a year (at 5¼%), it would earn $52,500. In a bank that compounds interest every day (also at 5¼%), it would earn $53,898.58. The difference is more than a thousand dollars! And the second year the difference would be even greater, and the third year even greater than that.

As you can see, figuring compound interest can be tedious and time-consuming. For that reason, no bank (or author) wants to figure it out by hand, or even with a calculator. But computers can calculate compound interest in seconds. Before computers, few banks compounded interest daily. That's one of many reasons to be thankful for computers.

Checks and Checking Accounts

Back in the days when people used gold as money, wealthy merchants often left their gold with goldsmiths who could store it safely. If a merchant, let's call her Mrs. M., wanted to give one ounce of gold to Mr. D. as payment for polishing her doorknobs, Mrs. M. might write a note to her goldsmith, Mr. G. The note would have a date at the top, Mr. G.'s name and address below that, and then a message that might go something like this: "Pay 1 ounce of my gold to Mr. D." Mrs. M. would sign the note and give it to Mr. D., who would bring it to the goldsmith to collect his pay. Notes like these were the first checks.

In the United States today, money is in dollars, not gold, and people store it with banks, not goldsmiths. But it is still possible to write a kind of note that tells your bank to give a certain amount to someone else. These notes are what we call checks. Americans write about 35 billion checks a year.

If you look at a check, you will see that it closely resembles a letter. Like a letter, it has a date at the top, the name and address of the bank to whom it is being sent, and a message telling that bank to "pay to the order of Mr. Horace Huggable one thousand dollars." In everyday language, that simply says, "Give Mr. Huggable one thousand dollars of my money." And, like any letter, the check closes with the signature of the person who wrote it.

If you want to be able to pay for things with checks, you must first deposit money in a checking account at your bank. Unlike savings accounts, checking accounts usually pay no interest because the bank does not hold your money for a long time. Instead it uses your money to pay the people to whom you have written checks.

When our Cheerful and Willing girl, let's call her Grace, hands the salesman a thousand-dollar check for his hippo, Mr. Huggable takes the check to his bank, which then sends it to a large clearinghouse. This clearinghouse is called the Federal Reserve Bank (most people call it "the Fed" for short). The Fed is actually a bank for banks: all around the country, local banks deposit their money in an account at the Fed, just as you deposit money in an account at your local bank. When the check to Mr. Huggable reaches the Fed, the Fed deducts $1,000 from Grace's bank's account and adds $1,000 to Mr. Huggable's bank's account. Then it sends the check to Grace's bank, which deducts $1,000 from her account. Grace's bank sends the check back to her along with a statement telling her that she now has $1,000 less in her checking account than she did before she bought the hippo.

As you can see, writing checks requires banks to do a lot of work, so banks often charge their checking customers for each check they write. Most people think the convenience of writing checks is worth the small charge.

Loans

To buy Gloomsby Hall, the Cheerful and Willing helper had to borrow $50,000 from his bank. The bank gets the $50,000 from the deposits its customers have put into savings accounts. Since the bank is paying interest to its savings customers, it must charge interest to its loan customers. In fact, the bank charges more interest to people who have taken loans than it pays to people who have deposited savings. This way, the bank makes money. Like pet shops, Ferris wheel companies, and movie theaters, banks are businesses, and all businesses must make money.

The interest rate charged for loans varies from bank to bank. It also changes from day to day. When you are looking for a loan, it's a good idea to look for the bank with the lowest rate. If the interest rate is too high everywhere, wait a while—maybe it will go down in a few months, or in a year or two. Perhaps Gloomsby Hall will have been sold by then, but it's also possible that Baroquebury Mansion will come on the market.

You may be familiar with another form of loan. When you purchase something with a credit card, you are actually taking out a little loan. You don't have to pay for the item right away because the bank that issued your credit card is automatically lending you the money to buy the item you have "charged." A few weeks later you will get a bill from the bank telling you to pay back the loan. Usually you won't have to pay interest if you pay back all of the loan right away. If you don't pay it all back, the bank starts charging you interest on what you owe. The interest on credit card purchases is very high. Credit cards look simple, but they can be an expensive way to shop.

Income Tax

The cheerful and willing workers of Cheerful and Willing, Inc., earned five dollars for baking a cake, one hundred dollars for transplanting a tree, and fifty thousand dollars for building a bridge. However, they may not be quite as cheerful once they realize that they won't get to keep all of their earnings. That's because all earners must pay a portion of their income, called income tax, to the government. Nobody *likes* to pay income tax, but most people realize that the government must collect taxes in order to provide the many services we expect—roads, schools, parks, airports, courts, even the army and navy.

Since part of your income goes toward taxes, you'd really need to earn more than a thousand dollars to have a thousand dollars. And you'd have to earn much more than a million dollars to put a million in the bank. In fact, you must pay income tax on the interest the bank pays you because interest is considered income, just like the money you make from painting a pot or mowing a meadow.

Will a Million Dollars in Pennies Really Stack Up 95 Miles High?

To find out without actually stacking that many pennies, you can measure a smaller number of pennies and use your answer to figure out exactly how high a million dollars' worth of pennies would be. Ready?

Measure a stack of fifty pennies. It's three inches high. Since there are twice as many pennies (one hundred) in one dollar, a one-dollar stack of pennies would be twice as high—six inches. How high a stack would ten dollars in pennies make? Ten dollars is ten times as much as one dollar, so a ten-dollar stack would be ten times as high as a one-dollar stack—sixty inches (10 x 6 inches = 60 inches). How many feet is that? There are twelve inches in one foot, so we must divide 60 by 12 to find out: 60 inches ÷ 12 inches/foot = 5 feet. The same procedure can tell you the height of a hundred-dollar or a million-dollar stack of pennies. Let's look at the million-dollar stack: 1,000,000 x 6 inches = 6,000,000 inches; 6,000,000 inches ÷ 12 inches/foot = 500,000 feet; 500,000 feet ÷ 5,280 feet/mile = 94.7 miles. In this book, we rounded off 94.7 miles to 95 miles. You can check the height of nickels, dimes, quarters, and dollar bills in the same way. Measure a manageable stack, multiply to figure out the height for the number of coins or bills you're interested in, then divide to convert your answer into the most useful unit of measure (feet, miles, etc.).

How do we know that a million dollars in quarters would weigh as much as a whale? Again, we must weigh a smaller number of quarters and then calculate what a million dollars' worth would weigh. Four quarters (one dollar's worth) weigh about 0.8 ounces. Since there are sixteen ounces in a pound, we divide by 16 to convert to pounds: 0.8 ounces ÷ 16 ounces/pound = 0.05 pound. In a million dollars there are a million times as many quarters, so the weight would be a million times as much: 1,000,000 x 0.05 pounds = 50,000 pounds, which is the approximate weight of many kinds of whales, including the sperm whale. (The largest blue whales, however, can be five times as heavy as that!)

The most difficult calculations in this book have to do with volume. It helps if you understand geometry, but the principle is the same: pour a known quantity (say, two hundred nickels, or ten dollars' worth) into a container whose volume you can calculate. My nickels filled a frozen-juice can 2.5 inches across to a height of 3.25 inches. To find the volume of a cylindrical container, multiply height by π (3.14) by radius (half the diameter) squared: 3.25 inches x 3.14 x 1.25 inches x 1.25 inches = 15.945312 cubic inches. To turn this into cubic feet, divide by twelve cubed, or 1,728 (the number of cubic inches in a cubic foot): 15.945312 cubic inches ÷ 1,728 cubic inches/cubic foot = 0.0092276 cubic feet. In a million dollars there are 100,000 times as many nickels, so multiply this by 100,000: 922.76 cubic feet. A standard school bus interior is about 28 feet long, 7.5 feet wide, and an average of 5.75 feet high, a total interior volume of 1,207 cubic feet—so our nickels would leave room for the seats and the driver.